THE SEN

comes to the country

Brigid Chapman

Illustrations by Angela Webber

First published in 2007 by CGB Books
53 South Street, Lewes BN7 2BU
Tel: 01273 476622

The moral right of Brigid Chapman and Angela Webber
to be identified as author and illustrator
of this work has been asserted

ISBN 1 873983 02 6

Designed and typeset by CGB, Lewes

Printed and bound by CPI Antony Rowe, Eastbourne

CONTENTS

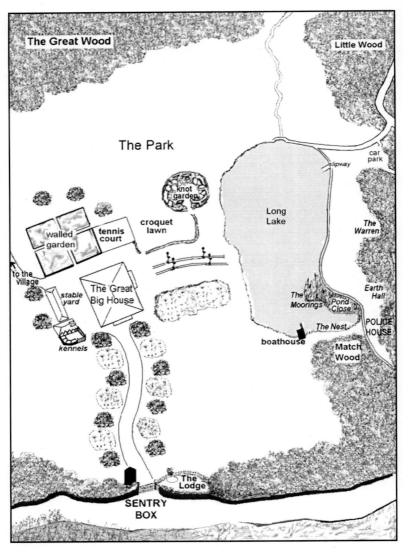

Sketch plan showing the sentry box at the gates of the
Great Big House – and part of its 365 acre estate.

1

WHO GOES THERE?

THE sentry box was lonely. It was used to the bustle of London life and all the red buses and black taxis it could see over the heads of the scarlet-coated soldiers who always stood in front of it.

Now it was in the country – it had no idea where – and was surrounded by nothing but landscape.

All because it was made of wood and was considered by the Health and Safety people to be a fire risk.

'Long past its sell-by date, let's get rid of it,' they said, and bundled it on to the back of a lorry and sent it off to an auction of army surplus stores and equipment at Hammersmith.

There it was bought by a

retired colonel who planned to put it in the front garden of his bungalow at Angmering-on-Sea in Sussex.

'Somewhere to sit in the summer, dear girl.' he said to his wife.

'Don't be silly, Cyril. There isn't room,' she said. 'Find someone to take it off your hands'.

Which is how the sentry box came to be standing inside the gates of the Great Big House, ready to do duty as a temporary ticket office for the car park when that stately home opened to the public.

All it could see was scenery – woods, hills, a lake, lawns, far too many flower beds, lots of lumps of statuary, and in the far distance, the spire of a church.

The small house on the opposite side of the drive did not look as if anyone was living in it. There were no curtains at any of the windows

that the sentry box could see, no lights came on when it got dark at night and there was nobody about to shout 'HUGOSAIR' or 'STAN TEASE' or any of those other magic words the soldiers used to say to each other.

The sentry box yawned. It was not only lonely, it was bored. For something to do it started to sing:

> *Stamp, stamp, TENSHUN,*
> *Standing guard must be done.*
> *Left, right. STAN TEASE,*
> *Altogether, if you please.*
>
> *Stamp, stamp, pass friend,*
> *Eyes front and knees bend,*

Quick march,
By the right,
Soldiers STAN TEASE
Every night. . .

'That's a fine, military song,' said a voice with something of a squeak in it.

'HUGOSAIR' said the sentry box, amazed to find that it was not alone after all.

'Why, a friend, of course,' replied the voice.

The sentry box looked everywhere. It did 'eyes right' – nothing. 'Eyes left' – nothing. 'Eyes front' – still nothing.

'Try eyes down,' said the voice. The sentry box looked at the ground and there, standing in front of it, was a small brown mouse wearing a white coat and a scarf with horses' heads on it.

'I am Millicent Housemouse and live over there in The Lodge,' it said. 'I used to share my kitchen with Kathryn Catte and her nephew, that fer-rightful Furr-Red.

'They moved to the Great Big House when the old

general died last winter. Mr Kemp, the lodgekeeper, is the caretaker there now and he looks after the dogs in the kennels and the pigeons in the loft'.

'I am so glad to meet you,' said the sentry box. 'I haven't seen a single soul since I arrived by lorry from London yesterday and was dumped here.

'I've been most terribly lonely . . .'

'There's no need to be lonely in the country,' said the mouse firmly. 'There are animals everywhere. Why look, there's Sandra. She lives at the Drey, just behind The Lodge'.

She beckoned with a small brown paw to the red squirrel that had appeared from among the trees on the other side of the drive.

'Come over here, Sandra, and meet my new friend,' called the mouse.

'Sorry, can't stop,' shouted the squirrel 'I'm having lunch at the Kennels with Leonie . . .'

'She's not a natural redhead, you know, she dyes it,' the mouse whispered as the squirrel dashed off up the drive.

'She's really a grey squirrel. One of that lot that

came over from North America and drove most of the British red squirrels out of their dreys'.

'The grey squirrels in the trees in St James Park didn't have pretty tufted ears like your friend, Sandra, has,' said the sentry box, glad to be able to contribute something to the conversation.

'They're not all her own ears, they're hair pieces,' said the mouse waspishly. 'She went to the beauty salon run by Kathryn Catte's Siamese cousin, Madame Lou Pin, and paid a fortune for them.

'Now that she is best friends with Leonie La Brador, who has a pedigree as long as your arm and is very much top dog around here, Sandra is doing everything she can to conceal her origins.

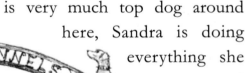

'Oh! Look, there is Leonie now, standing at the gates of the Kennels'.

The sentry box did an 'eyes

left' in the direction the mouse was pointing but it could only see the lime trees and flower beds that lined the right hand side of the drive leading to the Great Big House.

'I am afraid I can't see any kennels,' it said. 'My field of vision is limited to a semi-circle of what is in front of me'.

'Never mind,' said the mouse. 'You'll meet Leonie when she comes to see Sandra. Last winter that stuck-up squirrel was always over at Earth Hall with Fiona Fox but that all stopped when Fiona Fox started Keep Fit  classes with Kathryn Catte and they didn't invite Sandra to join them.

'But I can't stay talking all evening. I am going to have a word with Sailor Sam at Pond Close. He's giving our History Society a talk on heraldry next week and I want to know what time he wants us down at the boathouse and if Deirdre Duck is supplying refreshments or are we to bring our own'.

There was a rustle of leaves and the mouse was gone.

'STAN DEESIE,' said the sentry box to itself.

It had never met a mouse before, nor had it seen a squirrel with dyed hair and false ears, nor heard about dogs with French sounding names giving parties in their kennels or cats and foxes that did Keep Fit.

And who was this Sailor Sam who was going to give a talk about heraldry?

'And where is Pond Close?' it said out loud.

'At the eastern end of the Long Lake, not far from the boathouse,' croaked a deep voice.

'HUGOSAIR?' gasped the sentry box.

'Police Constable Albert Frogge. Shall I advance and be recognised?'

There was a plop and a large, green frog carrying a black truncheon in one hand and holding his cap on his head with the other, landed on the floor of the sentry box.

'Do you mind if I conduct a search of your premises?' it said.

'I am in pursuit of that cat burglar known as Furr-red.

Jack Rabbit's aunt, Jade the Spade, says he's been at the mint again and done a lot of damage'.

Now the only Mint the sentry box knew anything about was the Royal Mint in London where coins of the realm were made, as well as the banknotes that the soldiers were given on pay days. Surely Furr-red could not have damaged that?

PC Frogge had produced a magnifying glass and was studying its floor for paw prints when the sentry box felt a soft thud on its roof and something that felt warm and furry whispered:

'Don't think we've met before, squire. I'm Furr-red Catte.

'D'you want to buy some fresh herbs? Just the things for a tasty omelette and nice with salads. Can fix you up at the right price'.

The sentry box did not know what to do.

There it was with a cat burglar on its roof and a police frog searching its floor.

'STAN DEESIE,' it cried in desperation.

PC Frogge at once clasped his hands behind his back and rocked to and fro gently on his heels.

'Could do with a bit of a rest,' he said. 'Been on my feet all day. Mind if I sit down and eat my sandwich?'

Without waiting to be given permission he settled comfortably on the seat at the back of the box and started to munch the squashed fly sandwich he had taken from under his cap.

'Purr-um, purr-um,' whispered Furr-red. 'It's a bit awkward with old PC Frogge being here. I think it's about time I made myself scarce.'

He jumped from the roof of the sentry box to the top of one of the big stone pillars on either side of the gates. From there he leapt on to an overhanging branch of a tree and disappeared among the leaves.

The sentry box felt as if its hat had blown off.

'Did the cat burglar do a lot of damage to the Mint?' it asked the munching police frog.

'Stripped a whole row from the garden of that lodge over there,' replied the frog, licking a greenfly leg off his lips. 'He'll be back for the basil later, mark my words.'

'Who is Basil?' asked the sentry box.

'It's not a who, it's a herb – like mint, but with a different taste and smell.

'Well, I think I'll call it a day. That wretched cat will have got rid of the stolen herbs by now. Let me know if you spot him lurking round The Lodge'.

'How do I get in touch with you?' said the sentry box. 'I can't move from here.'

'I'll ask the pigeons to drop in on you daily. Since the post office in the village closed those birds have been delivering all the letters on the estate'.

The frog hopped off up the drive towards the

Great Big House leaving the sentry box even more puzzled than before. Nothing at all like this had occurred in London. The policemen that rode past the palace on big bay horses were real policemen, not frogs who ate greenfly sandwiches and called the Royal Mint a herb.

It came to the conclusion that it had a lot to learn about life in the country but at the moment there was nobody about to answer its questions.

'STAN DEESIE' it said and began to sing itself to sleep:

I've met a little mouse
Who has a kitchen in her house.
She had an awful had a lot to say
About a squirrel from The Drey.

I've had a cat upon my head
Who's stolen from a flower bed
And a police frog on my seat
With greenfly sandwiches to eat

Oh! country life is very strange,
I miss the streets and people.
Here there is no guard to change
So now I'll go to sleeple . . .

2
THE COBWEB CLUB

WHEN the sentry box woke up it was early morning and the birds in the trees were singing for all they were worth.

Their voices in the soft morning air sounded so very much sweeter than the grumbling 'coo-er, coo-er, coo-er' of the London pigeons.

Then there was another noise. A sharp 'chink' as if pieces of metal or glass had been clapped together.

The sound seemed to come from where the sentry box's left ear would have been had it had one. It was also aware that there was something pressing against its side.

'Eyes left' it whispered to itself, and carefully peered in that direction.

It was astonished to see that a ladder had been placed against it and a fox was steadying it while a cat, holding something very carefully in one paw, was climbing down.

A black Labrador in a smart green anorak had a tray in its mouth ready to receive what the cat was carrying.

'Got an absolute beauty,' said the cat as it reached the ground and placed an object on the dog's tray.

'That is splendid. You are clever with the clamp, Kathryn,' mumbled the dog. It was having difficulty in speaking with its mouth full of tray.

'That makes three in one morning, not too

bad for beginners,' said the fox, writing busily in a brown leather-covered notebook.

'Now we must measure them all carefully and count the number of lines. Perhaps we should have a competition for the biggest and the best one'.

'With a prize for the winner,' said the cat.

The sentry box could contain its curiosity no longer.

'TENSHUN' it said, so loudly that the cat dropped the bag it had just picked up, the fox fell back with the ladder and the tray flew out of the dog's mouth and on to the ground.

Two squares of what looked like clear glass landed on the floor of the sentry box but did not break.

There was nothing on them that it could see.

'Oh, you did make us jump,' said the dog. 'Now I have dropped it and it's probably ruined. I am sure it would have been one of the biggest and best.'

'Never mind, Leonie,' said the fox. 'Serious collectors never bother about little setbacks. You'll find plenty more'.

He picked up the two pieces of Perspex and looked at them closely.

'Yes, it is very damaged, I'm afraid,' he said.

'As you startled us into dropping this specimen perhaps you can provide us with another one tomorrow,' he added, looking first at the sentry box and then at his watch.

'At about the same time, I think.'

'STAN DEESIE, STAN DEESIE,' said the sentry box. 'What am I to provide?

'What are you collecting?'

'Why cobwebs, of course,' said the fox. 'Haven't you heard of the Cobweb Collectors' Club?

'I am the secretary, Philip Fox. Kathryn Catte is the treasurer and Leonie La Brador is a new member. That cobweb under your roof was her first find'.

'I am so very sorry,' said the sentry box. 'I didn't mean to startle you. I am a stranger here. I have been in London all my life and don't know anything about the country'.

'We'll soon put that right,' said the fox firmly.

'When I get home I will check with our chairman and, if he is free, we will have a meeting of the Cobweb Club here tomorrow afternoon so you can meet the members'.

'Oh! Philip, if you see Dickie Birde will you tell him I have done those photocopies of his *Paw and Claw Guide to a Great Estate,*' said Kathryn Catte.

'I tried to telephone him this morning to say they were ready but I could not get through'.

'There has been nothing but trouble with the utilities at Pond Close since Deirdre Duck started watching those gardening programmes on television,' said Leonie. 'Sandra told me that the

Swanns are furious about all the decking she has had built round The Nest . . . '

'And look at the trouble there was when she had that water feature made,' said Philip Fox. 'I warned her against using old Walter Vole's cowboy firm of builders. Those rats put in a pump that overloaded the electricity supply and everything stopped working'.

'And Deirdre was so upset that she flew into the overhead lines and had to be cut free,' said Leonie.

'Wonder what she'll think of next?' said Kathryn 'But we mustn't stay here gossiping. We have things to attend to.

'Do you mind if we leave the ladder here with you for the moment?' she said, looking up at the sentry box 'I will ask Henry Hare to hop over later and take it back to the Lodge'.

'Only to happy to be of use,' said the sentry box.

'And please, Miss Catte, could I buy one of Mr Birde's guide books. I would so much like to read it.'

'Do call me Kathryn,' purred the cat. 'And I will get Dickie to bring you a copy with the compliments of the Cobweb Club'.

'She'll forget, you know,' said Leonie La Brador confidentially when the fox and the cat had gone. 'She's terribly absentminded. Look, she's left her handbag behind'.

'Put it inside, I'll keep it for her,' said the sentry box. 'If you've got a moment could you tell me more about cobwebs and why you col- lect them?'

'I know very little about them,' said Leonie. 'I've only just joined the club. 'Dickie Birde is the expert and what he doesn't know Sailor Sam does.'

She waved her tail in farewell and walked away.

The sentry box smiled to itself in the sunshine. It was

looking after a handbag and a ladder, and it had been told to produce a cobweb by tomorrow morning.

Once it had found out exactly what a cobweb was it felt sure it would be able to produce one. It started to sing again:

Stamp, stamp. TENSHUN
What are cobwebs
Are they fun?

Where will I find one
What do they do?
Are they red,
Or white,
Or blue?

'I'd say they were white?' said a voice. 'Or a silvery grey, ye ken.'

'HUGOSAIR?' asked the sentry box.

'Why Hamish McGander, of course.'

The sentry box had been doing its 'eyes left, eyes right' drill but it could not see anyone.

'I've been listening to ye singing for a wee while,' went on the voice. 'I didna want to interrupt, ye ken?'

The sentry box did not ken, and it did not liked being talked to by a Scottish accent it could not see.

'TENSHUN,' it said, firmly. 'Advance and be recognised'.

'Och aye, I will. Miss Catte sent me for the ladder. Henry Hare couldna get here. He's giving Fiona Fox a piano lesson at the Form Room'.

From behind the trunk of a lime tree in the drive wadd-led a well-dressed goose.

He had a pink and grey McGander tartan cap on his head and was wearing a silver buttoned covert coat. Under his left wing he carried a shotgun with its barrels pointed to the ground.

'You won't be able to carry the ladder as well as your weapon,' said the sentry box. 'Leave it with me. I'll look after it for you. It's unloaded, I trust.'

'Aye, it is that,' said the gander. 'I've been banging away at the clays with those gundogs from the Kennels and used up all my cartridges'.

He put the gun carefully inside the box, collected the ladder and walked off with it.

The sentry box was beginning to feel more at home every minute. It knew all about cartridges and clay pigeons for the soldiers would often talk about the prizes they had won in regimental competitions.

It carried on with its song:

STAMP, STAMP, TENSHUN.
I've met a goose whose got a gun
And I'm going to get a book
Into which I can look
To find out where Earth Hall is sited
To which Sandra's not invited.
And where Deirdre Duck is wrecking
The surroundings with new decking.
Will the Moorings be included
And the Form Room — so secluded.

But I also need to know
Exactly where the cobwebs grow.
I must provide one by tomorrow
Or it will all be grief and sorrow.

Never mind, I'll do my best
But first I'll take a little rest . . .

3

THE MEETING

THE sentry box's little rest lasted well into the following morning.. The country air was certainly having an effect on its sleep pattern.

By the afternoon it still had no idea what a cobweb was and there had been no one around to ask. It had hoped to get some information from that Fer-rightful Furr-red who it had spotted padding quietly along the top of the garden wall with a green hosepipe coiled over one shoulder.

However, the moment it called out 'STAN TEASE – PLEASE' the cat had jumped down from the wall and disappeared.

Was Furr-red acting suspiciously, the sentry box wondered. Should it send a message by pigeon to the police house at Pond Close. Or was the cat just returning a hosepipe that it had borrowed from The Lodge.

Before it had time to make up its mind there was a flock of pigeons flying round it. One carrying a mail bag in its claws called out:

'Anything for Pigeon Post, guv? Bert Frogge told us to check with you each day'.

'No, er. . . no, not at the moment,' said the sentry box, rather bewildered by the birds.

'All right, see you tomorrow,' said the last bird as they all flew away.

A few more hours passed and then there was another whoosh of wings and the biggest bird the sentry box had even seen dropped to the ground in front of it.

'HUGOSAIR?' it gasped.

'Did I startle you, my dear fellow?' said the bird. 'I am Richard Gray-Heron, chairman on the Cobweb Collectors' Club.

'I want to thank you for inviting us to meet here

and to give you my *Paw and Claw Guide to a Great Estate*. Kathryn Catte said you would like a copy'.

'Thank you so much, sir' said the sentry box, deeply impressed by the commanding presence of the magnificent bird.

'Would you be kind enough to sign it for me?'

'Of course, my dear fellow,' said the heron, taking a pen out of the bag from which he had produced a copy of the guide.

'What name shall I put?' he asked. "To the sentry box" sounds a bit impersonal.'

'The soldiers always used to call me "Sid",' said the sentry box shyly.

'Splendid,' said the heron, and he started to write:
To Sid.

Welcome to the Great Estate— and read all about it
Richard Gray-Heron

September 2006

'How about that?' he said as he held the booklet up

so that the sentry box could read the inscription.

'Shall I put it on the seat?'

'Yes, sir, please sir, thank you, sir'

'Oh, Sid, do stop calling me sir' said the heron. 'You're not in the army now, you're in the country and we're a friendly lot down here. Everyone calls me Dickie – except old Phil Fox when he's got his club secretary's hat on'.

'Yes, sir – er . . .Dickie;' stuttered the sentry box as the club members began to arrive.

Among the first was a rather flustered Kathryn Catte, followed by Philip Fox carrying a large brief-case.

'Hello, Dickie' said Kathryn as she rushed up to the sentry box. 'Oh! There's my handbag. Leonie said I'd left it here'.

She lifted the bag off seat, searched through it to find her glasses, put them on her nose and began sorting through the bundle of papers she had in her hand.

'Good afternoon, Mr Chairman,' said Philip Fox,

offering a paw to the heron who was talking to the Swanns, Hamish McGander and the other birds who were all jostling for space on the roof of the sentry box.

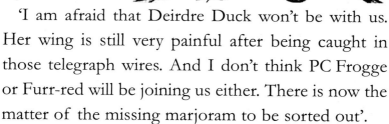

'I am afraid that Deirdre Duck won't be with us. Her wing is still very painful after being caught in those telegraph wires. And I don't think PC Frogge or Furr-red will be joining us either. There is now the matter of the missing marjoram to be sorted out'.

'I like a sprig of marjoram on my salad,' said Millicent Housemouse to Judy Rabbit, as she bent down to pick up some of the leaflets that Baby Bunny was tossing out of her push chair. 'It grows very well in the garden at The Lodge'.

'I prefer basil,' said Judy. 'Now stop it, Baby, or mummy will be cross.

'Thank you, shall I take that?' she said to Millicent who was pouring over the holiday brochure she had picked up.

'Are you really going away for the winter, Judy. How exciting,' twittered the mouse, reluctantly releasing the brochure.

'If you are looking for a tenant for The Warren I know someone who might be interested.'

'No, we are not spending the winter abroad. That is strictly for the birds,' said Judy. 'Jack's Aunt Jade asked me to give these brochures to Deirdre Duck. She wants then for the swallows who have been spending the summer at Pond Close. Pity she won't be here'.

'Leave them with me. I'll give them to her on my way home,' said Philip Fox as the heron called out:

'Now gather round, everyone, and give a hearty Cobwebbers welcome to our new friend, Sid.'

There was much clapping of claws and flapping of

wings and cries of 'good to have you with us, Sid. Do you miss London?' and – from Sandra Squirrel who had climbed on to Leonie's back – 'tell me, Sidney, how many times have you seen the queen?

'STAN TEASE, STAN TEASE' said the sentry box, confused and touched by the warmth of this welcome. 'You are all most kind . . . But please, Mr Chairman, before you start the meeting, will some-one kindly tell me what a cobweb is.'

'Let us put that question to the members,' said the heron. 'Will you start the ball rolling, Mr Secretary.

'It's a spider's lunchbox,' said Philip Fox. 'That's the description I have in my notebook. Anyone got anything to add?'

'Or it could be its breakfast tray,' said Leonie La Brador

'Or its dinner bowl,' said Kathryn Catte. 'It all depends on what time of the day it is. I think I have a picture of one in this file. Yes, here it is'.

'We are going to get some T shirts made and this is the logo we are going to have on them.'

'But what does a spider look like?' asked the sentry box as it studied the picture that Kathryn was holding up for him to look at. 'I've never seen one'.

'Ooh! look, there's one under your roof,' squeaked Millicent Housemouse.

The sentry box did a quick 'eyes right' and saw, at the very edge of its roof, a small greyish-bodied blob with eight legs, hanging from what appeared to be a very thin piece of cotton.

It dropped like a stone for another six inches or so and swung itself across to the white painted wooden side of the box. It stuck there for a few seconds before scrabbling up to the inner edge of the roof, trailing another thin piece of cotton behind it.

Again it paused, as if to tie a knot, or fix something, then crossed to the outer edge of the roof again, leaving another loop of thread behind it. The spider continued working this down-across-up-across pattern while everybody watched it, fascinated.

The sentry box hardly dared to breath. It could not believe its luck. Philip Fox had told it to produce a cobweb and here was a Blob making one, in just the right place and at just the right time. Never mind that it tickled terribly whenever the Blob's eight legs made contact with its side – it would laugh about that later.

'At this time of day I suppose we should call that a tea plate,' said Millicent when the spider had finished work and settled down on the edge of its web. 'Can I claim it as I saw it first?'

'Shouldn't it be Leonie's?' said Sandra Squirrel. 'She was promised a replacement for the one that was lost yesterday morning.. And it is in the same place.'

'It cannot be anyone's while it is in use,' ruled Dickie Birde. 'It would not be fair on the spider. After all that work it deserves its tea or its dinner'.

'Quite agree, Mr Chairman,' said Philip Fox. 'Cobwebs have to be empty before they can be clamped. Rather like cars, really. It is all made quite clear in Rule Seven'.

He leafed importantly through his briefcase, found a copy of the rules and showed the page to Millicent.

'But we haven't adopted these rules yet,' she said.

'Let's agree them now,' said the chairman. 'All those in favour raise a paw – or a wing or whatever,' he added looking at the Hamish McGander and the Swanns inquiringly.

A forest of paws waved in the air – and the birds indicated their agreement by raising their bills.

'Now, those against?

'Good, then that's settled.

The web cannot be clamped until the spider has finished with it'.

'Point of order, Mr Chairman. Shouldna we decide who can have it when the spider has finished with it?' asked Hamish.

'I saw the spider first,' squeaked Millicent.

'I found the one that was there yesterday,' growled Leonie.

'But we have all watched it making this web,' said Philip Fox. 'So we could all lay claim to it.'

'Quite right,' said the chairman. 'I propose we leave it where it is – with Sid. Those in favour?'

Once again paws and bills were raised in agreement.

'Fine, that is carried. Any other business? No? Then I declare the meeting closed'.

The stately heron stepped out of the sentry box, bowed its beak and said: 'We can rely on you to look after the cobweb for us, can't we, Sid, old chap? Stand guard, so to speak'.

'Yes, sir, of course , er – Dickie,' it stuttered in reply.

The club members moved off, singly or in pairs, until the sentry box was quite alone.

'TENSHUN' it said softly to itself, looking proudly at the cobweb with the Blob in it under its right arm.

It prepared to stand guard all night to protect the club's property.

To keep awake, it sang softly to itself:

Halt, halt, HUGOSAIR?
Eyes left, eyes right
Eyes everywhere

Shoulder arms, by the right.
I must be prepared to fight
Anyone who dares to try
To rob my spider of a fly

No one shall snatch
That web away.
I will guard it night and day,
Night and, (YAWN), day. . .

4

CAME THE DAWN

THE Blob was having its breakfast when the sentry box woke up at seven o'clock the next morning.

It was making short work of the second of the two small flies that had entangled themselves in the bottom left hand corner of the web during the night.

'That's torn it,' said the sentry box as it looked at the broken strands.

'The club's cobweb has been damaged while it is in my care.

'And I have been asleep on duty'.

While the sentry box was trying to remember what the sergeant used to say to the soldiers on guard at the palace about dereliction of duty – and what the punishment for it was – the spider finished the fly and folded its napkin neatly.

It knew it had taken a risk spinning another web in the place from where its previous one had been stolen. But the hunting was so good here. The two flies it had for breakfast had been really tasty . . .

'Why did those animals clamp my lunch box yesterday?' it asked itself. 'What could they want with it?'

'It's a good thing I was not in it at the time or they would have had me too'.

The Blob decided to look around for an alternative and, hopefully, a safer site.

It climbed on to the roof of the sentry box and scuttled as quickly as its eight legs would take it up the steep slope to the top.

There it paused to admire the view. The flowers were still in bloom in all the beds bordering the drive, the leaves on the trees were taking on the tints of autumn and the black arrow weathervane on the stables showed that the wind was from the west.

All was quiet and peaceful at the Great Big House but what was going on at Pond Close? It could see the sunlight glinting on water where there should not be water.

'I expect that dizzy duck is installing a swimming pool,' muttered the Blob as it walked carefully along the top of the roof and dropped down on a thread of silk in front of the sentry box.

It peered inside and almost fell to the ground with fright at what it saw when it looked up to the underside of the roof.

Sitting at the edge of a straggly and dusty web was a very large spider indeed.

'Ooooh!' squeaked the Blob.

'Hello,' said the spider. 'Nice of you to drop in. 'I'm Lil Legs from London. Came down in a lorry with this old sentry box. You from rahnd 'ere?

'Er, er, yes.' squeaked the Blob, overwhelmed by the sight of the first house spider it had ever seen and more than a little confused by its accent and the shape and size of its web.

'Bit small, ain't yer' said Lil, focussing all her eight short-sighted eyes on the Blob.

'That's because I am a common or garden spider,' explained the Blob. 'And because I'm a boy. My seven sisters are quite a bit bigger than I am. They are spending the summer at Seaford'.

The female house spider, Tegeneria gigantea, *can be up to 18mm long.*

'How'd they get there?' asked Lil. 'Haven't seen much in the way of road transport since I've been down 'ere.'

'No, they flew,' said the Blob., beginning to feel more at ease with this large friendly lady from London.

The male garden spider, Araneus diadematus, *is 8mm. The female reaches 12mm.*

'They went on that strong north-wester we had in April . . .'

'Yes, I remember,' interrupted Lil. 'It blew the busby off one of the guards.

'He had to chase it all the way down the Mall. It didn't arf make us laugh.'

'It must have been quite a sight,' said the Blob. 'We only lost a few trees down here.

'Nothing like it was in October 1987 when us garden spiders were blown all over the south of England. My mother's family came all the way from Dorset . . .'

'Don't just hang about out there. Come on in and tell me all abaht yerself,' said Lil. 'Swing over to that cross beam. There's a ledge at the end of it that runs rahnd the inside of the roof. I'll meet yer there.'

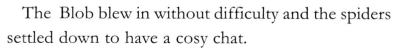

The Blob blew in without difficulty and the spiders settled down to have a cosy chat.

The sentry box, quite unaware that it had cobwebs and spiders both inside and out, was worried about what action the club members would take when they saw the damage that had been done to the cobweb that had been left in its care.

What could it say in its defence?

That the Blob tore the web getting those flies for its breakfast? Or that it was torn when that cat burglar, Furr-red, tried to steal it?

No sooner had it thought of Furr-red than there was the sound of purring and something warm and furry brushed against its left leg – or where its left leg would have been had sentry boxes had legs.

'HUGOSAIR?' it asked.

'There is no need to shout,' said a Siamese cat, putting the two smart cases it was carrying on the ground.

'I am Madame Lou Pin, beautician and hairstylist. I have an appointment with Miss Sandra Squirrel who lives at the Drey.

'I don't usually do house calls, you know, but she was most insistent. She said she would meet me at her ground floor storeroom to save me having to climb up to The Drey with these cases. Where do I go from here?'

'The Drey is in one of those trees over there, behind The Lodge,' said the sentry box. 'There's a guide to the Great Estate on the seat and there is a map in it'.

'Never mind that,' said the cat. 'I haven't got my reading glasses with me. I am sure I can find it. Behind that house over there, you say . . .'

Madame Lou Pin picked up her two cases and walked across the drive into the garden of The Lodge.

'Hope she won't hurt her ankles in those high heels,' murmured the sentry box as it watched the Siamese cat depart.

It was sorry she had not brought her reading glasses and opened the guide book Dickie Birde had given him. He was relying on visitors bringing it outside to look at so he could read it over their shoulders. That is what he had done when tourists had consulted their guide books when they came to look at the palace in London that he had guarded for so many years.

The next arrivals were Leonie La Brador and Millicent Housemouse.

'Good morning, Sid,' they said. 'We've come to take a photograph of our cobweb. We know it belongs to the club but we think of it as ours'.

'Oh! There are some torn strands at the bottom,' said Leonie, looking at the cobweb beneath the roof of the sentry box.

'Never mind. It shows the web is in use – and the spider will soon mend it'.

'How do you know that?' asked the sentry box.

'Yesterday you could not answer any of my queries about cobwebs.'

'She can now,'

said Millicent. 'I asked Furr-red to get a book about spiders from the library at the Great Big House. You can borrow it, if you like.

'And look what else Furr-red found for us,' she said, as Leonie took an oblong package out of her back pack.

The dog and the mouse unwrapped the package and showed the sentry box a gilt framed picture of a piece of purple silk on which the two words '*VIVAT LESPIDAR*' were embroidered.

'And I have borrowed Kathryn's digital camera. The one Furr-red gave her for her birthday,' said Leonie. 'He said he got it from a catty log but we all think it came from that charity shop in the village'.

Leonie put the picture down carefully, took a neat little camera from her backpack, aimed it at the sentry box and made some adjustments to the focus.

'Yes, the sun is on the cobweb so it is showing up

really well against those trees,' she said as she started clicking away with the camera to her eye.

Millicent continued to chatter – 'Kathryn says she will print the pictures for us on the new computer in the estate office. Its got a Smart card, whatever that is. Isn't technology marvellous?'

'With this one we can see at once what the pictures  look like,' said Leonie. She lowered the camera so the mouse could see the images as she scrolled through.

'Yes, they're fine. Now what about a few interior shots?'

'STAN TEASE, STAN TEASE,' said the sentry box. It had been standing smartly to attention, with 'eyes front', from the moment Leonie had produced a camera. That was what it had always done whenever tourists pointed cameras at it in London.

'Yes, please,' it said, as it relaxed. 'I hope it is not too untidy inside. No one has swept or dusted me out since I have been here'.

'It is a jolly good thing they haven't,' said Leonie excitedly. 'There's a huge dusty cobweb in the top left hand corner inside your roof'.

She focussed the camera on the web in the rafters and the two spiders it contained smiled sweetly at her and continued their con-versation, quite uncon-cerned by any flashes of light or the pres-ence of a large black Labrador.

'This is really wonderful,' said Leonie as she emerged back-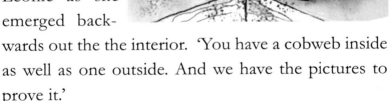wards out the the interior. 'You have a cobweb inside as well as one outside. And we have the pictures to prove it.'

She waved her camera triumphantly in the air and then put it in her backpack and picked up the picture of the motto.

'Where shall we put this?' she asked.

'Why not on that hook above the seat?' suggested the sentry box.

'Ooh, yes. Just the place for it', squeaked Millicent. 'Can you reach it, Leonie?'

'Hop on to my back, Millicent, and I will walk my front paws up the back of the box. 'Then, if you climb on to my head and go towards my nose you should be able to reach the hook and put the cord over it.

'I'll keep the frame in my mouth to keep the weight off the cord until you tell me it is safe to release it.'

When this operation had been completed successfully the dog and the mouse said goodbye and trotted off up the drive towards the Great Big House to get their pictures printed.

The sentry box was rather confused by all the activity that had being going on around it and inside it, but also very relieved.

Admittedly a cobweb had been damaged while in its care but it had provided another, together with the spiders who made them, and a framed picture of the club's motto. That was surely something to sing about:

EYES LEFT, EYES RIGHT
Ooh! I had a fearful fright.
When it was light.
The web the club left in my care
Was not all there . . .

In one corner it was torn
And I was feeling so forlorn
For I had been asleep on duty
And the committe would be snooty.
I was afraid of what they'd say
Or if they would all walk away.

STAN TEESE, TENSHUN
It was not the only one
Some kind spider in the night
Spun a web with all its might

Now I have two
And that will do.
Oompah, Oompah, ta ra ra
Tiddle diddle dee and la la la. . .

The sentry box tried to do a little dance for joy but it was firmly planted on a stone base and could only managed a bit of a wiggle of its middle.

'Did you feel that?' the Blob asked Lil as the beam on which they were sitting began to shake.

'I think I better go back and check if something has hit the outside of this box and damaged my web.'

'See yer later, lad,' said Lil. 'Think I'll 'ave a bit of a nap.

'Being up all night spinning a web don't arf take it out of you – and I don't just mean me silk.'

5

PROBLEMS AT POND CLOSE

SAILOR SAM was standing at the water's edge of The Moorings, his home by the reed bed, rehearsing the talk he was to give in the boat-house on Friday afternoon to the Great Big House History Society.

His audience was made up of some water boatmen who were scudding across the little creek by Pond Close as if they were racing from Putney to Mortlake.

They paid not the slightest attention to what the newt was saying about the armorial bearings of the families that had lived in the Great Big House since the days of Good Queen Bess.

The newt watched them with interest – and envy. If only he could scull about on the water with such speed and effortlessness instead of always having to swim through it to get to where he wanted to go. He remembered, as if it was only yesterday, that epic voyage on the water that had earned him the nick-name of Sailor.

He had been a very young newt, playing with his brothers and sisters in the reeds by the boathouse, when he was scooped up in a bucket that some children were dangling in the water from a pole with a hook on the end.

'Ooh! look what we've got,' they cried. 'It's a water lizard'.

The newt was in no state to contradict them for it was being poked and prodded with bits of stick.

'Leave it alone,' said a grown-up voice. 'How would you like to be poked in the ribs with a stick?

'We'll sail across the lake to where we left the car. There's sure to be something on natural history in that box of books we picked up from Mrs Gatley for the charity auction. With a bit of luck there may be a picture of this little chap in it'.

The newt in its bucket of weedy water was placed carefully in the bow of a fibre glass sailing dinghy and one of the two small boys held the handle to make sure it did not tip over.

The newt heard, but could not see, the mainsail and jib being hoisted, accompanied by much slapping of canvas and the creak and squeak of mast and halyards.

Then all was quiet, except for the ripple of the water against the hull as the boat skimmed across the lake, powered by a gentle westerly wind that registered Force 3 on the Beaufort scale.

The little newt loved every single minute of it. However, all good things must come to an end and its journey did with a bump and a scrunch and a rocking motion that almost tipped it out of its bucket.

Then the bucket was carried ashore and taken

along the bank to where a car was parked. The newt heard doors being opened and closed and papers rustling. Then it was peered at by a pair of horn-rimmed glasses, and the grown-up voice announced:

'Yes, here we are – the Reverend J G Wood informs us on page 278 of his Boy's Own Book of Natural History that the little creature we have here is *Triton Cristatus*, the Great Crested Newt.

'And look – here is a picture,' continued the voice. 'Apparently the male reaches a length of 150mm and feeds principally on tadpoles and worms. The female lays her eggs on the leaves of water plants and ties them to them with regular knots . . .'

'Can we keep our newt, Dad?' interrupted a young voice.

'No,' replied the adult. 'We haven't got an aquarium – or even a garden pond. We will sail back to the boathouse and return this young *Triton Cristatus* to its friends and relations'.

With a lot of 'ready abouts' and 'mind your head'

and other nautical noises from the captain and crew, the dinghy tacked back across the lake and the bucket was emptied gently over the side close to the reeds.

When it was reunited with its brothers and sisters the newt, whose name was Sam, described its voyage to them in detail – at length, and repeatedly.

It kept saying how marvellous it was to be on the water as well as in it, always adding:

'Did we sail – or did we sail – or did we sail – or did we . . .'

Sailor Sam's reverie was cut short by a crash, a splash and a rush of water that carried him away from the reed bed almost to the bottom of the lake.

As he came to the surface to draw breath he was knocked on the nose by a baulk of timber. A few seconds later there was some distressed

57

quacking and Deirdre Duck plopped into the water almost of top of him.

'I'll sue those wretched rats for every cent they've got,' she said angrily. 'One minute I'm reading the paper on my new decking; and the next minute I'm up to my beak in water, my new television is at the bottom of the lake and I've lost the sling that supported my injured wing'.

She then noticed that Sam was holding a water lily leaf to his nose.

'Oh! Sam, I'm sorry to go on so. Are you badly hurt?'

'Dough, Deirdre. Just a dock on the dose,' said Sailor Sam. 'Had dunt we better go an idspect the damage?'

They swam through the floating debris to the bank and joined PC Frogge, the Swanns and Henry Hare, who was on his way to play the piano for Baby Bunny's birthday party at The Warren.

The surroundings of The Nest were a shambles. Planks of broken timber from the decking were drifting about on the lake and the garden on which

Deirdre had lavished so much cash and care was in the most terrible mess.

The water feature – a cascade rippling down over steps of natural and napped flints into a small artificial pool with a fountain in the centre – was no more.

In its place was a raging torrent that had scoured away everything in its path as it tumbled into the lake.

Then, to the amazement of the watchers, it stopped as suddenly as it had started. The torrent turned into a trickle and the trickle to an occasional drip.

'That's good' said PC Frogge,

putting the mobile 'phone into which he had been speaking, back under his cap. 'The tank has emptied. The fire brigade said that it would take about ten to fifteen minutes'.

'What tank?' asked Henry Hare.

'There's one over there in Match Wood,' said the frog, pointing with his truncheon towards the trees that covered the hills behind Pond Close.

'Old General Stoars had it put in after the fire started by that picnic party in the hot summer of 1976'.

'That's where the water came from for my feature,' quacked an angry Deirdre Duck with feathers flying.

'Walter Vole advertises garden design by experts so when those rats said it was quite safe to run a garden hose from it for the cascade I natu-rally thought they knew what they were doing'.

'This doesn't look much like a garden hose to me,' said Henry Hare, who had

climbed up the bank and was looking at a big brass nozzle from which
came an occasional drop of water.

'This is one of
those proper
high pressure
hoses – the sort
of thing used by fire-
men to quell riots and
douse burning buildings.
No wonder it washed most of your garden away'.

'I wonder if it did any damage to the boathouse?'
muttered Sailor Sam. 'The History Society's meeting
there on Friday – I better go and have a look. . .'

He slipped into to the lake and disappeared.

His departure went unno-
ticed for all eyes were
focussed on the hose. The hare
was about to pick the nozzle up
and examine it more closely but PC
Frogge stopped him.

'Don't touch it,' he shouted. 'There may be finger-
prints. Someone must have changed the hoses. . .'

He walked off into the wood and emerged a few

minutes later looking worried – but interested.

'Something funny's going on,' he said. 'General Stoars had two hose outlets fitted to that tank up there last summer. One for the fire brigade's hose and the other for an ordinary hosepipe so his gardeners could water the young trees they had planted without having to carry cans up from the lake.

'That must have been the one the rats used for your water feature, Deirdre, but its gone and only the high pressure hose is connected. I wonder who did that?'

The Swanns had been silent throughout this exchange. As they were mute swans no one had expected them to speak but Deirdre Duck was rather upset when they walked away without so much as a wave of the wing or click of a beak to express their sympathy.

'Snobby lot,' she said. 'Just because they have royal connections they think they own Pond Close.

'And as for their two cygnets, Sigismund and Cynthia, I wouldn't trust them an inch'.

'Neither would I,' said Henry Hare. 'They're far too friendly with that Fer-rightful Furr-Red.

'Jade the Spade had to chase all three of them out of the herb garden at The Lodge when she working there one day last week.'

'If you see Jade at Baby Bunny's party will you ask her to get in touch,' said Deirdre. 'I'm going to need a lot of help getting this garden back in shape'.

'Yes, certainly,' said the hare. 'I hope for your sake Walter Vole is well insured. Since Jade won that award at Chelsea Flower Show she has doubled her hourly rate, you know'.

'We can't be sure that it is old Walter Vole's work-men who are at fault here,' said PC Frogge to Deirdre when the hare had hopped away. 'They would have no reason to change the hoses over and destroy the water feature they made for you.

'You have paid their bill, haven't you?' he added as an afterthought..

'Of course I have, Bert,' said Deirdre. 'After Walter Vole had agreed to deduct the price of the pump. It was the wrong voltage and we were all without electricity here for hours'.

'I will put it down as "person or persons unknown" in my report and I will continue to investigate the matter,' said PC Frogge.

He then put on his cap and climbed up the bank to examine the nozzle of the high pressure hose for paw prints – quite expecting to find those of THAT CAT . . .

6

GOODBYE BOATHOUSE

DOWN in rather cold water near the bottom of the lake was a very worried water spider.

Argyroneta aquatica – call me 'Argy'– had set up home in the lilypond at The Nest in the spring, and was planning to sleep there through the winter in the underwater retreat he had made.

He was jolly proud of the air conditioned bell-shaped structure, which he called Tinkle Towers. It had taken him countless trips to the surface to collect the amount of air needed to fill it so he could live there in comfort.

And now it was gone – washed away, as he had been, by an unexpected rush of water.

Or was it? He had anchored Tinkle Towers pretty firmly to that lily root so it might still be there.

'I better go and have a look,' he said to himself and swam to the surface.

'Hello, Argy, did you get caught up in that flood?' said a familiar voice from the reeds as he neared The Nest.

'Yes, I did, Dolly,' said Argy to *Dolomedes fimbriatus* – at 22mms the largest spider in Britain.

'It washed me right out of Deirdre Duck's lily pond and into the lake. I came back to see if the home I'd built for the winter is still there'.

'Let's have a look,' said the raft spider, who had been waiting for a hovering damsel fly to settle within striking distance.

It climbed to the top of the bank, stood on tiptoe, held several legs to its eyes and looked towards the gash carved in the hillside by the torrent.

'There's no pond there now, Argy,' said Dolly as she returned to the water's edge.

'And no sign of your old home. I'm so very sorry.'

'These things happen,' said the water spider philosophically. 'There's plenty of time for me to build another Tinkle Towers. 'Can you recommend a suitable site?'

'What about in the old boathouse,' said Dolly, pointing with a front leg at the derelict wooden structure. 'Surprised you don't know it. Lots of local societies meet there – including those Cobweb Collectors.

'They will probably make you an honorary member if you move in.

'Come on, let's go and have a look round'.

Dolly and Argy swam along beneath the wooden jetty and into the old boathouse. It was not a pretty sight.

The torrent that had wrecked Deirdre's garden had crashed through the corner of the north east wall and washed away most of the staging. Only an upturned tea urn remained of the refreshment bar that had been built in an alcove where oars had once been stored. It was floating about in the water, together with posters advertising forthcoming attractions and bits of broken wood.

Sitting in the midst of the wreckage, on the remaining rung of a ladder that led into the water, was Sailor Sam — still holding a leaf to his nose.

It was in these — for him — comfortably wet surroundings that he gave his talks on history and heraldry. But not any more.

Now there was nowhere for his paw and claw audience to sit or perch in safety. Nowhere for Deirdre

Duck to dispense the refreshments she had promised to provide for his Friday afternoon talk.

A poster advertising his talk was still on the notice-board by the door. He better let the History Society know it would have to be cancelled unless an alternative venue could be found.

And that would not be easy. He knew of no other premises in waterside surroundings that could accommodate a membership that ranged in size from Millicent Housemouse, to his tall friend and fellow historian, Dickie Birde.

**GBH
History Society**

Talk by Sallor Sam
on:
**𝕿𝖍𝖊 𝖍𝖊𝖗𝖆𝖑𝖉𝖗𝖞 𝖔𝖋
𝖙𝖍𝖊 𝕲𝖗𝖊𝖆𝖙 𝕭𝖎𝖌
𝕳𝖔𝖚𝖘𝖊**

AT THE
OLD BOATHOUSE

FRIDAY, SEPTEMBER 12
2.30PM

'Pity I'm the sort of amphibian that needs to keep wet. . .' he muttered as he swam back towards The Nest, hoping that PC Frogge with his mobile phone would still be there.

Suddenly there was another crash and splash and a swirl of water that tumbled him almost to the bottom of the lake.

When he surfaced he saw there was something missing from the skyline. The boathouse had gone.

Only a short length of jetty on the east side was still standing. The rest of the old black tarred build-was being blow about on the surface of the lake by a blustery west wind.

'Could I sail– or could I sail – or could I sail on one of those?' thought Sailor Sam for an instant.

Then he pulled himself together, remembered he was now an adult newt with responsibilities, and climbed on to the bank to look for Deirdre.

He found her in the remains of her garden, talking to Jade the Spade. There was no sign of PC Frogge.

'Did you hear that crash, Sam?' they said. 'The boathouse has blown down.'

'I know, I was there,' said Sam.

'What happened?' they said. 'Were you hurt?'

'Not this time' said Sam. 'Luckily I got out with seconds to spare. The water torrent that ruined your garden had smashed a huge hole in the east wall and tore out all the staging. I'm not surprised that the roof caved in'.

'What are we going to do for a hall now?' asked Jade, scooping up several pages of plans and putting them in one of the five pocket of her gardeners' apron.

'I've been booked to talk to the Flower Club there next Saturday about autumn planting and I was so looking forward to your talk on heraldry, Sam.

'I want to make a bank of shield-shaped beds with the arms of all the Great House families picked out in plants'.

'What a wonderful idea, Jade,' said Sam. 'Heraldry in horticulture. Grow your own family tree.

'You could start with the arms of Osward St Oars who came over with William of Normandy in 1066.

The blazoning is:

'*On a shield vert, a rowlock proper between two crossed blades or, with roundels azure . . .*'

'I could do that easily enough,' interrupted Jade, sketching busily.

'Two oar-shaped beds of buttercups and the two circles above them of bluebells within a shield shape of bright green grass. The rowlock could be made of

metal and connected to a sprinkler system to water the bed in high summer.

'How about something like this?' she said, showing her drawing to Sam.

'Stop it, stop it, you two,' quacked Deirdre. 'Never mind the past — let's deal with the problems of the present.

'Somehow we have to let people know the old boathouse has been washed away and meetings that were to have been held there will have to be cancelled unless a new meeting place can be found quickly'.

'That's why I came,' said Sailor Sam. 'I hoped PC Frogge would still be here. He has a mobile phone'.

'Bert went up to Match Wood and then he was going on to talk to Furr-red,' said Deirdre. 'He won't be back at the police house for hours'.

'Pity those pigeons don't do an afternoon collection as they used to,' said Jade. 'I asked one of them why they had stopped and he said most people are now using e-mail.

'When I asked him what e-mail was he replied – rather rudely, I thought – "get a life granny" and flew away'.

'If only my left wing was working properly it wouldn't take me any time at all to fly across to The Lodge and let Millicent know what has happened,' said Deirdre. 'She would soon spread the news around'.

'As your air mail is out I suppose it had better be a case of *'run, rabbit, run,'* said Jade, collecting her papers and picking up the measuring tape she had been using.

'I'll leave these designs with you, Deirdre, so you can look through at your leisure. Let me which one you like best and then I can give your an estimate. I'll collect the rest of my stuff on my way back'.

'My goodness, I wish I could get around on the ground – or in the water – at that speed,' said Sailor Sam to Deirdre as Jade the Spade scampered off up the hill towards The Lodge.

'Just look how that rabbit can run'.

'She's pretty fit for her age, I agree,' said Deirdre rather condescendingly. 'I suppose it's all the digging that does it.'

They both walked to the water's edge and looked sadly at the remains of the boathouse.

'I suppose if your talk is cancelled, Sam, I won't have to provide any refreshments,' said Deirdre.

Then high in the air above the lake they saw a large bird with a bag in its beak.

It was Richard Grey-Heron on his way back from delivering copies of his *Paw and Claw Guide* to the bookshop in the village.

They waved and called to him and he glided down and landed on the ground beside them.

'What has happened?' he asked as he looked around.

'Deirdre, my dear, your lovely garden's been quite washed away – and where is the old boathouse?'

The duck and the newt told the heron all about the torrent from the water tank and explained that the matter was now in the capable hands of PC Frogge who was, probably at this very moment, questioning the prime suspect – Furr-red Catte – at the Great Big House.

'It might not be THAT CAT,' said the heron. 'When I flew over Match Wood this morning to get some aerial pictures for my next book, *Birde on the Wing* – do you like the title? – I saw some men in yellow jackets walking around the water tank and examining the hose connections'.

'I took quite a few pictures of them. Let's have a look and see what they were doing'.

Dickie Birde reached into his bag, produced his digital camera and scrolled through the display.

'Ah, here we are. Yes. They must be going to empty the tank through that high pressure hose. 'Look, there . . . You can see them running it along the ground'.

'And they've coiled up that garden hosepipe that fed my water feature,' quacked Deirdre.

'We better let Bert Frogge see these pictures straightaway,' said the heron. 'Or he will be bringing poor Furr-red Catte back here in chains. I'll go and find him'.

'Oh, I do wish my element was air,' said Sailor Sam as he watched the heron fly majestically away.

7

SAVED BY SID

THERE was something niggling at the back of Dickie Birde's mind as he winged his way towards the Great Big House, where he hoped to find PC Frogge and Furr-red.

Then he remembered. He should have looked at what was left of Deirdre's pond to see if that water spider's winter quarters were still there.

He had spotted Tinkle Towers last week and intended to take an underwater photograph of it and amaze the Cobwebbers at their next meeting.

The object of the heron's deliberations – and his friend, Dolly – had been washed to the other side of the lake when the old boathouse had collapsed.

'What is going on around here?' grumbled Argy.

'Do you think its something to do with this climate change and global warming they're forever going on about?'

'Doubt it,' said Dolly. 'Climate's always been changing. More likely to be something to do with that dotty duck and her home improvement schemes'.

They were drifting along at the edge of the reed bed by The Moorings when Argy suddenly shrieked:

'Look, Dolly, there is Tinkle Towers'.

On top of a water lily pad that had been washed into the reeds was the remains of the bell he had spun and filled with air.

'Let's see of we can shift it,' he said. 'If we can slide it into the water it won't take me long to sort out the ventilation'.

The spiders climbed on to the water lily leaf, put their shoulders and four legs to Tinkle Towers, shouted 'Heave-ho' in unison and began to shove . . .

As Dickie Birde neared the Great Big House he spotted PC Frogge hopping down the drive towards the sentry box.

He was leading Furr-red by a chain which was linked to a pair of handcuffs that he had fastened round the cat's neck like a collar.

The heron swerved to the left and glided to the ground by the gates as the police frog and his prisoner approached them. At the same time Jade the Spade and Millicent Housemouse came running across from The Lodge.

Everyone started talking at once.

'Have you seen what's happened to the boathouse, Dickie?' said Jade.

'Now we've nowhere to hold our meetings,' squeaked Millicent. 'What are we to do?'

'I think this photograph will clear up the question of who changed the hoses, officer,' said Dickie Birde, holding out his camera.

'I have the miscreant here,' said PC Frogge to the

heron. 'However, he claims that shortly before mid-day today he was on the wall by the Lodge and this sentry box called to him'.

'TENSHUN' shouted the sentry box.

It had dozed off after its dance for joy, happy in the knowledge that it had more than fulfilled its duty of care for cobwebs. Faced with a sudden barrage of sound it reverted to military mode.

'Yes, Constable, I can con-firm that I saw Furr-red on the wall over there at about midday. He had a green hosepipe coiled over his shoulder'.

'Oh, well done, Furr-red, you found it. Where was it?' interrupted Jade the Spade

'At the back of the stables,' said Furr-red. 'Mr Kemp had been using it to wash his car'.

'A likely story,' said PC Frogge.

'STAN TEASE,' said the sentry box, and the frog immediately did so.

'You have a picture to show this officer, sir . . . er – Dickie,' said Sid, still very much in charge of the situation. 'Please do so'.

'What time was this taken?' said PC Frogge, as he examined the picture.

'11.23am. The time is on it,' said Dickie.

'My call to the fire station was logged at 11.35am. 'That's when the torrent stopped,' said the officer.

He turned to his prisoner, unlocked the handcuffs and gave him a friendly pat on the shoulder.

'You're free to go, Furr-red. No hard feelings, just doing me duty'.

'That's all right, Bert, glad its all worked out,' said the cat, and it settled down to wash its neck where the handcuffs had been.

'Thanks so much for sorting things out for us, Sid, my dear fellow,' said Dickie Birde. 'Now can we pass another knotty problem over to you?

'The boathouse has gone the Cobwebbers are without a headquarters'.

'So are the Histsoccers,' squealed Millicent. 'And we

have a most important meeting tomorrow'.

'I was booked to speak to the Flower Club there on Saturday,' grumbled Jade. 'That'll have to be cancelled and I suppose I shall have to forget about my fee'.

Sid had a sudden thought. He would volunteer.

'Why not make me your head-quarters, sir . . .er – Dickie,' he said to the heron. 'You will find the cobweb you put in my care is safe and there is another one under the roof inside. Please inspect them'.

'Sid, my dear fellow, what a splendid idea. I see you have an appropriate motto already in position. Where did that come from?'

'Furr-red found it and Leonie and I put it up,' said Millicent.

'Did Furr-red now?' said PC Frogge looking at the cat. 'I wonder where he got it from?'

'Came from a charity shop, Bert,' said the cat. 'And I've got the receipt'.

'Another likely story. Well, I suppose I better go and find those men in yellow jackets. Thank you all for your kind co-operation.' The frog saluted and hopped off through the iron gates.

'Now the law has left us where did you find it, Furr-red?' asked Dickie. 'That motto is most interesting. *Vivat Lespidar* – long live the spider.'

'I found it in a black bag in a skip at the the tip and gave it to Auntie Kathryn for the club,' said Furr-red.

'Hmm' said Dickie. 'That doesn't get us any further. I wonder if Sailor Sam knows any families round here with a name like Spyder or perhaps Le Spidar. I'll ask him at tomorrow's meeting'.

'But how will he get here – and where will he speak from?' said Millicent. 'You know he can't be out of the water for more than a few minutes'.

'He can use the lily pond at The Lodge as a platform,' said Jade. 'Come on, Furr-red and show me where you put the hosepipe and we'll top it up'.

'But how will he get here?' squeaked the mouse.

'Leave that to me, ' said Dickie Birde. 'I know just what to do. Thanks for everything, Sid. You've saved the day – see you tomorrow'.

The heron flew off with its bag in its beak.

'I must advise the members of the new venue,' said Millicent. 'I do hope our speaker will be here'.

The sentry box watched the worried mouse bustle across to The Lodge.

It shared her concern. For how was Dickie Birde going to get Sailor Sam all the way from the waterside at Pond Close to the lily pond at The Lodge.

The spiders in residence were wondering much the same thing.

'I do 'ope that 'e gets 'ere orl right,' said Lil to the Blob.

'I reely want ter know more abaht that motto'.

8

OPERATION AIRLIFT

ON his way home to the heronry on the edge of Match Wood Dickie Birde had called at The Moorings to discuss with Sailor Sam his plan to get him to the lily pond at The Lodge.

The newt had been delighted that a new meeting place had been found – and one with a platform on which he, as the speaker, would be in his element.

He had agreed to be ready for collection at 2.45pm the following day and in the meantime would see if he could find any references to a family named Spyder in his archives.

The heron had then dropped in at The Nest, told Deirdre Duck that PC Frogge was now in pursuit of the two men in yellow jackets, and examined the remains of her lily pond. There was no sign of *Argyroneta aquatica* or its winter quarters.

It was now 2.30pm on Friday, 2 September and time for Operation Airlift to get under way.

Dickie Bird collected his bag, which was hanging on a nearby branch, emptied the contents into his nest and covered them with twigs.

He had noticed that the other occupants of the herony were all out fishing so there was no one to keep an eye out for those marauding magpies.

'So much for Neighbourhood Watch,' he thought as he glided down to the lakeside. He would have something to say about this lapse in security at the next meeting.

Sailor Sam was in the water by the The Moorings waiting to be airlifted to the Lodge.

He was looking forward to the trip but feeling a bit uncomfortable in goggles and a flying helmet and with a parachute strapped to his back. But Dickie Birde had been most insistant about such safety precautions.

'Hello, Sam,' said the heron as it walked along the bank trailing its bag in the water by the reeds. 'Climb aboard and fasten your seatbelt'.

Sam swam down into the submerged bag, which had gathered up some weed and a water lily pad. He quickly surfaced, hooked his left arm round one of the handles and shouted – 'Let's go . . .'

The heron stretched out its neck, lifted the bag out of the water, flapped its huge wings and flew off towards The Lodge.

Sam was ecstatic.

This was far better than sailing across a lake in a bucket of water in the bow of a dinghy. He could see for miles, instead of a few metres. Look, there was the Great Big House – and the famous knot garden that had been designed by Lady Penelope Stoars in the early 1900s.

He did not

know that he had a fellow passenger and it was a very angry water spider.

Argy, with Dolly's help, had pushed Tinkle Towers into the lake, topped up the air supply and settled in for some well deserved rest.

Suddenly his home had been scooped up in a plastic bag and he was now being jiggled about in swirling water for the third time in two days. Where would he end up this time?

Argy parted the water weed by his front door and found himself gazing at the tail of a Great Crested Newt. And what was all this blurry whiteness and the flapping sound it could hear above the rushing of the wind? Then there was a sudden plop and a bump and the sound of voices.

'I've got it, Dickie,' said Jade. 'You can let go'.

'Hello Sam, did you enjoy the flight?' she asked the newt as she helped him out of the bag. 'Let me take your parachute and helmet and I will put them with Dickie's bag when I've emptied it, so everything will be ready for your return trip'.

'Jade it was wonderful. Did we soar . . .or did we soar . . . or did we soar . . .' said Sam swinging around from side to side with his arms outstretched and his eyes on the sky.

'Oops! Sorry, Millicent, I'm still in flight mode,' he said to the mouse who had rushed up to welcome him.

'I hope you approve of the speaker's platform we have rigged up over there by the drive. It's a bit of an old ladder that I found at the back of the shed,' said Jade as the mouse and the newt walked off.

She then picked up the bag and emptied Argy and Tinkle Towers gently into the lily pond.

'That went very well, didn't it, Dickie?' said Jade to the heron.

'Better than I dared to hope,' he replied, for his keen eye had spotted the water spider and its winter quarters slipping down between the lily pads. He would bring his camera next time he came to see Sid.

'Millicent, this is marvel- lous,' said Sam. 'Far better than that old boathouse. How did you find it so quickly – and get all these posters put up?' he added as the mouse led him round to the speaker's platform in front of which his audience was waiting.

'We have to thank Sid for everything. There he is, by the gate.

'Coo-ee, Sid – This is Sam, our speaker. Sam – this is Sid,' squeaked the mouse at the top of her voice.

'No need to shout, Millie,' said Sandra, who was formally attired in hat and gloves and sitting on a stool by the pond waiting to greet the speaker. 'And as chair of the Histsoccers I should be performing the introductions, not you,' she added, rather acidly.

'STAN DEESIE,' said Sid. 'Did you have a good flight, sir ? . . . er – Sam,' it added after a warning 'watch it, Sid,' whisper from the heron, who was standing beside him.

'Wonderful' said Sam, his arms outstretched again. 'Did we soar, or did we soar, or did we soar . . .'

He then noticed the VIVAT LESPIDAR motto hanging on the hook inside the sentry box and he at once became the serious historian.

'May I see that please,' he asked.

Dickie Birde unhooked the framed motto and carried it across so Sam could get a close look at it.

The newt turned the picture over, released the clips at the back and took it out of its frame. He propped it against Dickie Birde's legs so he could study it closely.

'Yes, just as I thought,' he said. 'It is worked in spider silk'.

He touched the motto reverently then turned to Sandra and said:

'Madame chairman, may we please dispense with the usual procedure and have a general discussion about this important find?'

'Important find, yes, of course,' said Sandra. 'Has it a local significance? The Le Squirrelle family, perhaps? We came over with William of Normandy in 1066 you know,' she whispered to Leonie.

'I believe it to be of great local significance,' said Sam. 'But what is it doing here? I would have expected it to be in the science centre at the Royal Observatory at Herstmonceux Castle, or in the Imperial War Museum'

(*'Cor, lad, d'yer 'ere that?' said Lil to the Blob. 'Our silk at a science centre . . .)*

'Why? why?' chorused his audience.

'Because it is the motto of a company that makes telescopic gunsights using the silk produced by spiders to make their webs,' said Sam, lapsing into lecture mode.

'The silk has a diameter of about 1/200th of a millimetre and has the tensile strength of iron. This piece of embroidery has been worked in spider silk on a background of what I think is cotton or a fine linen.

'It is of great value for its rarity and artistry and is a well-deserved tribute to the suppliers of a material that has improved the accuracy of our ordnance.'

(*'What's 'e goin on abaht?' said Lil to the Blob. 'Wot's ordnance?'*

'Guns, I think, Lil, or rather, large pieces of artillery,' replied the Blob. 'Sort I things they used to shoot down enemy planes in the Second World War'.

'Coo, you don't arf know a lot for a little 'un,' said Lil.)

'Many humans are afraid of spiders. They are not aware that of the 600 species of *Arachnida* in this country there is not one harmful to them. Rather than harmful, they are helpful'.

(*'Not to us' muttered a flustered fly as it tried to escape from the web under Sid's arm. It had been drawn to the sentry box by the scent of the refreshments laid out by Deirdre, with the help of the Swanns, on the grass by the gate.*)

Before Sam could continue to lull his audience into a stupor with his eloquent display of learning the sentry box lapsed again into military mode and called out:

'TENSHUN. Caps off.

Three cheers for spiders:

Hip! Hip! Hooray!

Hip! Hip! Hooray!

Hip! Hip!

Hooray!'

Everyone hurrayed heartily in response, waving wings, paws, beaks and – in the case of Sandra, Millicent and Judy Rabbit – their hats and headscarves.

Lil and the Blob bowed gracefully from the roof of the sentry box

(*'Think I'll settle here as the natives are so friendly,' said Argy as he swam back to Tinkle Towers.*

'Cor! Blob, me lad. We're the celebs rahnd 'ere. We'll be on the telly next,' said Lil.

'Back in a minute, Lil,' said the Blob, making its way to its web in which the flustered fly had become even more entangled. 'My tea's on the table'.)

The Histsoccers and the Cobwebbers followed the Blob's example and moved *en masse* towards the refreshments that Deirdre Duck had provided.

Sid could never let an occasion like this go by without a song. He started to sing:

Eyes left, eyes right,
This is such a super sight.
Paws and claws are everywhere
And look, there is Madame Chair . . .

I was brought here from the city
Knowing no one, more's the pity.
But such a welcome they gave me
That this is where I want to be
Until my timbers rot away.

Well, that is all I have to say . . .

Vivat Le Spidar! Vivat! Vivat!
Country life is what we're at.
Oompah! Oompah! Boom! Boom!
I'm such a happy club room.